THE HETEROGON
Or the normal-shaped Man

By Mr Joe Ira O'Hara-Childs

A #Joetry Novel of Ideas

Acknowledgements

The author would like to thank the following people for their encouragement and support in completing this book: Eileen O'Hara, Sam O'Hara-Childs, Chris Childs, Laurie Lewin (technical support), Sarah Anne Proctor, Sky Smith, Andrew McDowell, Helen and Susan Widlake, Tomo Hakagawa; and Julia Cazorla-Harsant, for moral support, behind the scenes. This has been a long hard road, but I am finally here, and it's with great dedication and perseverance that this has been achieved. Thank you, in advance, for reading.

The Heterogon is entirely a work of fiction

ISBN: 9798844544347

PART ONE – HEFT

<u>Chapter 1</u>

Battlin' and believing,

Thrown away by the tawdry

Talentless freaks, ever at the edges

Fraying, I find myself absorbed even obsessed

And proudly found brown in merriment of

Song - gusty and gutsy and he's only one call

Away, from a lighter lightning fire on the edge

Of sanity,

And spells, and quells and all I could send across the Sea,

Not meant for general consumption (you and me)

And an entire day, meant to save, from a different time,

A scalped and quaffed and hollowed out race that even
in the pitch darkness we cannot find,

Wish I could be kind always, and the gaunt Brown
tricks, hair and bees-wire finds itself

Mirrored and matched in the lovely

Remembering of you - so many you's

As I come to think, and think to come - on eve

Of blissed remembering -

Still under the blister, bluster and odd ferment

There's a foundation of belief, of something Undenied,
something not sneering at the Heroes effort, and he
still believes, in match

Of mayhem and it cannot be allowed nor disavowed,
nor even defied;

He believes, and that is enough for now:

My friend you have to just breathe.

Felltown was vast in mindset though small in scale. Vast meaning the breadth of opinion and vagaries of perspectives, in the town lent it a decidedly rebellious nature to the place in all directions at once. It was true that Grant was an outsider, in some respects, and perhaps one very important respect, having not been born within the confines of the delineated town. He was an Eastman, another throwaway or stowaway from the ring of commuter towns that surrounded the Big C, known as Lewdsburg. Uncertain though he had been, on first arriving, he had found a way to settle into the confines and rhythm of Felltown – and liked it well enough, one particular denizen most of all: his romantic muse, Tessa Hartley.

"You monster," he said, appreciatively. A toothy grin then met him, icily warm.

<u>2</u>

Subtle offer,
Jump back,
Easy prey,
The laugh peeling off the raptured scab
Of a new day
Spent in secrecy (merriment) and a torchlight
To the silent fighters (holding sway)
I live, laugh and love
As the saying goes
Rampant, wallowing and colourful

Well-bred to meet the challenges of the
Towering, soaring ebony, the cloaked
Ivory, the teeming and squirming, role
Of a coat-of-arms madness,
Proffer a question,
The skills to pay the bills,
An unleashed life, an unravelling scroll
The meme and emoji never quite enough:
Sure you could say anyone is secret police
Or some such hidden artifice,
Of course if no one tries, then everyone
Fails, so it's best to put your life out there especially if
they aren't such uncertain
Times. , So quick I fall back
Blank at the storm
Do you remember when times were more
Certain,
In fact can we see that now in our mind's eye
Rao, rao, wow
Maybe the sky falls.

"You're a bloody wet fish, Grant!" said Jon.

Grant shrugged, indifferent, but neither confirmed nor denied. The town was in tatters. But a good start. An exhausted, and yet freshly-minted feeling, overcame Grant and his aura. Jon took no prisoners, hence his moniker "Bad Jon Diamond", a symptomatic antonym he had necessarily, decisively earned. As the town burnt with the mellow and yet sallow fires of May, a creeping feeling overcame your protagonist that something was about to unfold, develop and develop indeed him, through that fiery gauntlet, he evaluated with finality. Dylan Gentley, his Government name but more properly known on the street as Dellus Grange, Grant's best mate, was a perennial sit-back and wait it off type, just lean back and see what the day brings, and although they had been mess-mates and buddies many years, there was an admission between them: that the lack of ambition, and a lack of true creative expression of their friendship, was something they shared – although preferring to focus on the good times, sit back and watch it happen, was always an 'option' of course. Tessa Hartley was the optic muse to Grant, the demure object that pulled him in, and pushed him on in his erstwhile endeavors towards an end that he could necessarily foresee and accept, with all his heart.

Grant had loved her since he first saw her, but it was futile, instead she loved not him, indeed she loved the concept of everyone else that lived, it seemed. Bad Jon Diamond was the 'maddest, baddest' guy around, but he had his antecedents, particularly "Mad" Mannal Dune and his liege lord Ricka Bockley, even Rafique O'Shaughnessy belied a certain charm, and many who bolstered and manned the firmament of the town, heartily disapproved of his more rascalish behavior – some of his wild antics simply being 'beyond the pale'.

<u>3</u>

Opinions, blessed in the eye-storm,
Position of darkness, a place of scorn,
The nebulous and vexing eyes of the red
Hex you put upon me in the stalking summer,
Witched and woken up,
Missed and swollen up,
By all that you just might carry thru the storm;
The eyes glazing over beneath the oncoming
Dawn, The sorrowful and swallowing dawn.
Onset of a new emergence
A recovery out in the forest;
The eagles quick, the forest thick,
With all my sanity — that I could give
Replacing my mentality with a drip, drip, drip
Feed of a crab shell unfolding, and nothing new
beneath;
Onset of a new discovery -
What was lost in the fall -

Arguable now whether should be ever Replaced
And, in fact, who would want it to?
I guess you miss me
Because the ghost calls on -
The malbec, and merlot, and proud Don Juan,
Of another evening in twilight,
By sunset kissed- friends we could call
On any ship;
I guess I miss you
Because the ghost calls on,
Hairy, harridan, hale and horse,
Beneath it all , the moonlight bleaching the only
Scene
I could call home.
Onset of the emergence of something New,
Praise be, bless thee
And thanks to the Gods
It's you.

Later that day, Grant popped into the Garrulous Lizard, the neatly antiquated and excessively shabby, hipster café right at the end of Halcyon Avenue, on the turning with Jovial Lane. As usual he ordered the most sin-free beverage he could think of – something the proprietor called a 5-inch stoat monkey, and sat down by the window to digest, smoothly, and scroll his smart-phone slowly. The day was long that stretched out before him, and thoughts of Tessa floated in, and gushed out, of his mind intermittently, odds and evens. He hadn't seen her since that day outside Declan's, et al., the antiques shop, and wished very much for another convenient 'bump'. He daydreamed if she ever went to The Pub Inn, with her mates, Melanie Funtumble and that 'other one'.

<u>4</u>

So in the mistle,
Wanton thorns and little fantasies besides,
Heaven in a baked form,
And lines crossing light-time as lilies grow,
Spent thousands – afterthought – time catching the
noose around
Bending, beckoning neck,
Lost you, had, you, granted you the space, heck!

So your protagonist wandered out, he was due a meeting with Soothsay, and one with Rafique, though he adjudged the latter was no doubt caught up in the latest herbal batch to arrive in Felltown, the wisps and the ethers, so would be otherwise engaged, so he plumped for a routine check-in with the Brandelbaeke.

Soothsay lived in a cabin, at the border of someone's garden, and the perimeter fence that ran to the railway – she had claimed it "many moons ago" and in an old-style country way now had the right-to-remain, or in other words, squatter's rights. The air was thick with a green mist – and a heavy boom to the atmosphere suggesting a full moon, though Grant hadn't checked in a while. He sometimes got out of synch with the celestials; Felltown grabbed him by the balls and distracted him from the creamy, tidal luminary's movements, at times and he kicked himself for not knowing; it wouldn't do to be ignorant going into Brandelbaeke's bower.

Soothsay was out to meet him in the dusky lane, of course, and the heavy leaves around her, framed her face like a cat's silhouette: indeed the air and aspect of the moment felt decidedly feline. Grant outstretched a manicured paw, Soothsay simply stared, unblinking, and pierced him with her eyes.

"So you've fallen out with Bad Jon, have you?"
Grant sniffed, "Again" she said.
"Yeah, me and Jon you know, its unhealthy, messy, borderline criminal" he paused, refocused his eyes on an oak leaf "and I don't want to follow him to the grave, particularly", he said.

"There's always room for rascals, Grant, and room for rascal-ing; you'd do well to remember your cheeky, sly side in all this 'merciless pursuit of Tessa' thing", she demurred. "Remember to have some fun", she added.

Grant pulled back on an elastic band pinned to the wall, and watched it twang back into place, "Still, I do have to refocus my mind, you see", he said, "Characters like Jon don't exactly lend one respectability, or indeed simple self-respect".
"I've drank more units in a week, than I did for the entirety of last year", he added almost in proud resignation. She pierced him again, and sunk low into a dusty yet multicoloured meditation chair, and he thought he heard her mutter "palatial".

"Robert's been round" she changed the subject, "did these blinds for me, don't you think they look lively, and lovely?" demurring.
Grant didn't, but muttered "Robert, yes, a great handyman, useful guy to have on the payroll for you, you still do his tarot – educate him in the ways of the Fae?" His voice seemed to suggest, etc, but he let it hang there, and waited for Soothsay to purr out her reply.

"Well, he has skin the game, you see, and Lord Ricka, that stubborn mule, has given him the nod, so it looks like he'll be moving up the world, tradesman badge, council seat, lock stock and the whole lot, "she said.
Hmmm, Grant wondered, don't know how this helps me, but maybe the moon isn't full, Soothsay is being pretty wayward, vague even, perhaps the energies he'd sense hadn't been quite so much of the 'intense variety'.

"You've thought about the vector of how next to approach Tessa?"

She didn't wait for an answer, "Harness the power of Mercury in Virgo and Venus in Taurus, in its exultation, Grant: be adaptable, flexible, cater to her needs, not with servility but with conscious care – and that should see you right in the next step towards Union".

Grant mulled, and stared again at the oak leaf gently rustling around on the floor, "Digested, and what's this about Robert, why do you always bring him up in our conversations?"

"He's what you will become, Grant, the evolution, the fully embodied".

"Okay, okay", he shrugged, "I will do that regards Tessa, it doesn't seem like a bad plan from the Brandelbaeke" he grinned, shot a look into her hazel-combined-with-Moorland-granite eyes, and turned to go.

"Remember, Grant" she said, "You must exercise discernment in all your actions from now on, those friends of yours…" The legitimate ones, she implied with a wink "Will not always lead you in the right direction; the pursuit of Tessa is your task, and your path, alone."

The leafy foliage seemed to envelop her once again, as he passed the border fence, and evening arrived.

<u>5</u>

*His fingers scraped at the wall of the well as he
descended
Nails screaming
How did he know? How could he know?
How would he ever know, deep doom,
What lay in the valley beyond the Doomed Valley?
Further from her now – ever – as two bright orbs
paced the sky
Red and green, saucy in their delight.*

It had transpired that some pretty monstrous things had
been happening in the outskirts of Felltown, some of
them actively instigated by Mannal Dune, Lord Ricka's
pet hunting hound. Bad Jon couldn't be found to rectify
the situation, so Grant, as he had a spare hour, head out
with a combined force of Dellus Grange, Robert Rettison
and Rafique, with his cat on a lead, both of whom could
fortunately be found for this excursion into the frontier.
Add to that, a rather nasty heads together by a pair of
alpha-seagulls, otherwise such docile loving creatures,
and you had a real afternoon of
pain/penury/exhaustion.

As they walked to the outer reaches of Felltown, they
spied 'Bad' Jon,

"There he is!" said Dellus. And there he was, pissing into a bin, clutching a freshly acquired bottle of red in his spare hand. Without being called, Jon turned and his generous member leaked copious badly-hydrated piss into the street. Rettison grimaced. It wasn't long before you found someone in this town, doing something unseemly; and this time it was Bad Jon. Dellus grinned toothily as they moved on.

Mannal Dune, to his credit, was prone to such aggressive flare-ups; combat with 'unwanted' interlopers, interlocutors or cultural dissidents was frequent, but it also came in intense patches, where it was clear Mannal had lost his mind, or gone off of his leash that was usually held so firmly by Lord Ricka.

On this occasion, he had broken through the fence and stolen the garden gnomes of someone he claimed had contravened an ancient local rite. As the party arrived, they found him bundling the offending articles and pieces of broken wood into an old wheelbarrow that he was due to wheel up to the inland cliff above Skye Head and throw into the 'abyss' proudly. Grant always consulted Soothsay in his head at times like this – and briefly pictured her showing him 'The Tower' card in one warty-weather beaten claw – he couldn't tell if this was a projection or a vision. For now, it didn't matter: she had done her work.

Grant braced himself – eyed the East and West, deep belly breath to centre and pulled himself up to full height, nearly on a level with Mannal. A moment passed.

Grant outstretched his left paw in a symbol of friendship
as he further approached the rabid Mannal, in hope that
on this occasion the latter was feeling congenial. Mannal
refused, and emitted something approaching Orcish. He
growled, Dellus backed off with a whimper. Rettison
strong-armed him and threatened to burn down his
caravan again if he did not desist.

Mannal momentarily stared at a point far-off, into the
unseen, and then switched to a jovial tone, dropping the
wheelbarrow as he did so. "You see the game last night,
eh, Grant?"

"Indeed," said Grant, not knowing what game Mannal
was referring to at all.
"Those women, eh, they can really ball in the upper
levels of it these days. Great stamina" he said, gesturing
incoherently with his well-knuckled hand.
"Yes sure," proffered Grant "Many things have
changed".
Mannal then went on to regale him with more stories of
how his mother had founded the governing body of the
sport in question, how he had personally been at the final
in the previous two years, how without him the entire
structure of international competitive sport would come
crushing down around our ears.
The others backed off, Dellus doing so with relieved
vigor, and said something about heading to the
Garrulous Lizard for a sly latte pick-me-up before hitting
the pub later. Grant assented but knew he would be
caught – amidships – in this conversation a while longer,
even as Mannal's smile became ever more convivial as he
waxed on.

There was always something sinister about being caught in a conversation with Mannal for longer than a brief 10 seconds, and Lord Ricka's pet hound was known to be safe only when talking.

Your protagonist thought of Bad Jon and his antics, and wished to be anywhere but here.

~

6

Improvising in isolation,
Are we just ions?
Can't make out an atom in an ocean in wistful misted
*bliss, *
Sundered and separate, we cast-
And gate ourselves out into the open aether –
Can we take charge, in birth or battle, of this doomed
untamed chaos
So you're tired of dumbing yourself down:
And I, in lies, seek truth,
Bent beneath the hammer and anvil of the deep
surrendered sooth –
Could give you that finality,
With set and rise:
Down to up, we are not just improvising in isolation.

Once again at the Garrulous Lizard, Grant was sat in the gossamer sling, Rettison at his side, quirkily jutting out from the repurposed pallet-wood wall.

"Yeah, so Rigorid was telling me the other day…" Rettison was saying.
Grant, wantonly preoccupied, did not have the energy to listen, simply gazed into his 6-inch cream weasel – he was feeling fruity with his order today – and mulled over the events of the past days. He felt the urge to go and see Soothsay again, get her to pull a tarot card, etc. And yet, seeing Tessa the other day with her friends walking along Jovial Lane, he was contemplating summoning up the courage to approach when she was with 'her pack' next time and putting forward the proposition of a day trip. Somewhere out of Felltown, to Fasterleigh in the east possibly, nowhere as far as the Big C – a new vibe, a fresh quirk; somewhere he guessed Tessa hadn't been in a while.
Still doggedly persevering with his Rigorid story, Rettison went on in hushed tones "so he said that Bad Jon's on his way out, new (big) boy in town, that Mannal Dune is up for electing – and coupled with his superior health, and ideologically dubious support of Lord Ricka Bockley, it's looking like a dead cert-"

Grant huffed, and swigged his weasel.

The ideological dubiousness Rettison spoke of was tribalism, memetic capture; tribalism had set-in in Felltown like some of the substrates of the firmament, so was very difficult to remove. Lord Ricka, or simply Richard to those who despised his grandiose airs, was indeed a chief proponent of this tribalism – a get them before they get me attitude – that served to defend and repel Felltown from and to Newcomers – giving it an air, even if outwardly tolerant, of a very deep set-in tribalistic spirit. Perish the thought; the town was ever besieged by inappropriate tribal outsiders.

Grant, for his part, was rather resigned to that fact; any half-listening to Rettison only served to reinforce the facts he already knew, Lord Ricka loved-to-hate the town, and 'Mad' Mannal did his dirty work for him, with vicious aplomb. It was the only way the doughty manservant found peace.

<u>7</u>

Scant on the fringes; lazy, lizardlike, in between.
Hold that marsh soft, keen
A little wisdom, and a little purring within – God's
redoubt is without –

Grant awoke in the middle of the night, driven by a loud bang. Thunder. He turned to look at his bed-side alarm clock. 3:06 am. A flash of light, as he turned to look beside him. Melanie Funtumble lay beside him in the bed; he had no idea how she'd gotten there. Judging from their shared denouement of clothes he assumed foul-play, and the doings of Bad Jon; he couldn't yet remember if he'd had a run-in with that particular rascal last night.

A stare into the darkness at the bottom of the bed: a half empty – spilled – bottle of whiskey lay on the floor. His glasses lay askew. Definitely. Foul play. Mischief. Antics.

*

Later that day, your protagonist Grant had tumbled out of the Garrulous Lizard and was up on Skyie Head with Dellus.

"Enjoying the view?," came a voice.
Grant, awakened out of his stupor, and turned to Dellus with a sheepy-eyed expression. "You've been like that for 10, no 11 minutes, mate", he said, proffering a hand to the great expanse that lay before them atop that summit. Ah, thought Grant, I've been in one of my trances again, wondering about Melanie, and how the woman had got there.
"True Dellus, sorry mate, just something happened last night – something let's say I didn't expect," Said Grant.

"Something you didn't expect", Parroted Dellus, then continued:

"Ah well mate, doesn't matter too much, when you've got a view like this: I text Rafique, he should be up 'n' along any minute", emitted Dellus. Grant breathed a sigh of relief. Anything to shake him from the Funtumble trance; Rafique would at least supply a lotion or potion to leaven his day's mundanity and they would necessarily get a breakdown of the latest American Football scores.

Silence followed again, and the vastness of the vast looking point suddenly took Grant's breath away.

He couldn't explain it. One minute he had been remonstrating with Mannal over on the Western fringe and then, he could only guess, Bad Jon must have interceded. She (Funtumble) had left gracefully enough; in fact Grant had told her to leave the door on the latch, as he left first and popped out for a quick one at the G' Lizard. All he could ascertain was chaos had promptly ensued after that incident with Mannal on the Western Fringe – no doubt it had involved whiskey hence the evidence in his room. His lack of awareness in such situations scared him at times – so obsessed was he with Tessa Hartley – and to have a quick-run in with Funtumble at a time like this. He wondered indeed if he was not crazy, and the cogs and gears of time, had indeed rendered him useless to the perils, and charms, of Felltown.

Then however – it all paled into insignificance that Mel Funtumble had woken up in his bed as he gazed out at the wondrous vista of Skye Head – and that Bad Jon had doubtless been involved; and that his 7 ½ creamed ferret at the Garrulous Lizard had done more than just woken his up from his whiskey fuelled haze, but acted as a total tonic to his rather overgrown psychological thicket.

Rafique sidled into view, a few minutes later – and Dellus met him with an enthusiastic fist-bump/gangster/urbanized hand-shake that was clearly rehearsed. Grant merely smiled, and thought of how once he used to be fun.

<u>8</u>

Crumbling at the seams
Yet silky and seamless
A thorough, enflamed, hedge, a boy caught and
lambasted,
And yet that streetlight, pointing at a cupboard
boisterously,
Wish you could have captured that sunlit moment
between our buried souls,
Hell claimed that peak While I watched, and Heaven
holds the deep dell Yet,
Branching, me
But before you it came,
That damaging storm and such an obsession cannot
last –
Breeze and morning light the light buffet of the vesper
on the
Oak leaf – oh how I wish I could give you these things
every day.
The Gods that hold this scene, they befit me.

A quick glance at Mannal Dune, a few hours later, told Grant everything he needed to know. As he sat out in the square, swigging clumsily a large Continental beer, it was evident the vicious attack dog had been subdued for now.

*

Later that day your protagonist, Grant, and the 'boys' were at The Pub Inn, when in walked this dowdy looking rugged fellow – strongly announcing himself as "Areo Nort-Rambabast, brave and handsome Explorer" to the astounded, nonplussed barkeep. He lanced out a sinewy, calloused paw. Grant and the lads, having been joined by Rettison, simply stuck to their Czech pilsners and stole a quick glance at the new man. He seemed to be searching for a welcome reception from the dewy-eyed sleepy locals. The man promptly glanced around the bar, and caught Grant's groups' eye.

"Evening," he said. "Areo Nort-Rambabast, brave and handsome explorer".
"Evening, champ, not heard of you," spoke Dellus quietly.
He proffered his big, bronzed hand once again, and Dellus shook his head as the barkeep had done – pithily implying that we don't do that around here.
Half a beat followed.
Grant stood, a new round of pilsners needed to be ordered.

The new man, Areo Nort-Rambabast, for the name could
not be forgotten, adjusted and stood adjacent to Grant,
catching his eye. The latter could feel a silent, internal
dick-measuring contest going on. Rettison huffed shiftily;
Grant improvised a shoulder pat, shoulder biff to the
man as he passed, making for the lacquered, bulb-lit bar.

*

Later, once they had moved to the Mucky Stable, and
forgone the Pub Inn for the time being, Grant mulled
over the events in the previous pub while he went
outside into the Spring rain for a quick puff of a straight
cigarette. This man, brave and handsome explorer, Areo
Nort-Rambabast clearly had an edge on the town:
something "to do" here, a mission, an objective, an
agenda. Hard to say what it was, at this early stage. He
thought he heard Tessa's voice from the silvery bar, a
high laugh in a sweet cadence. He steeled himself, puffed
his chest and took a deep breath.

Bravely, he adjusted his tousle of sandy front-quiff, and
re-entered the bar.

*

Well it seemed to have all worked out. Grant was four whiskies down, had been forced to improvise a tune on the bar's resident ukulele and had won three arm wrestles of the grueling variety. Areo Nort had backed off – the battle had been won for now. Sometimes, though, Grant was aware of a dim light of 'what was he fighting for?' but usually put those fears to bed by simply engaging with what he saw before him. Not an easy customer, Areo had fought to the last, but had now swooped off to the other late-night drinking spot the town had on offer, scampering off with his tail between his legs.

Grant, though dimly aware of the honor he was defending (Felltown's) and the reason for valor and dogged grimness in the face of an arrogant interloper (Areo) sometimes did get lost in the moment. The whiskies he'd drank (the Irish variety) had not settled easily on his stomach after all the pale ales and Pilsners – and his thoughts turned moodily to the Mel Funtumble and Lysander Rigorid situations, which he knew were linked, and acknowledge with a sigh.

*

Somewhere, deep in the night, Bad Jon howled wildly, adjusted his sunglasses and sou'wester and blundered straight into an oncoming dry-stone wall. His blood was up – reason again unknown.

<u>**9**</u>

*Battered and bewitched, yet becalmed
The icy malice of the full moon receding,
Castigated with castanets – and born before that big
red burning-
The hero is oneness with the shallow divot that allures
him,
And in nightmare and in peace, fashions his fastened
fathom
To that One, sticking, unremitting, beat…*

Grant and his cronies, or lieutenants, or flankers, perhaps cronies was best, had once again seen Felltown through the smoke, and bled or juiced the most out of the night's lemon. Longing for another liaison with Soothsay Brandelbaeke, Grant once again regaled the teeming stream of peace-flags outside Deglan and Espion's – the colours exploding in his brain, hungover as he was.

"Morning", chirruped a passing, what Grant guessed was, female.
"Yeah, uh, morning!', he ejaculated. Realizing only too late it was indeed Melanie Funtumble.

Dellus was down at the dairy, Rettison probably out in the field with his salty Dad, attending to some pressing agricultural issue: Grant's mind could only settle on Rafique O'Shaughnessy, for company, and so pondered firing the man a quick text to alert him of his arrival.

Rafique, was never busy as such, but always had something he was latterly obsessing over, some aspect of his matrix or system that needed maintenance or fixing; the cogs greasing, as he often said.
Grasping his 4.2 duck-horn, the latest creation procured from The Garrulous Lizard, Grant indeed made his way to the end of Jovial Lane, and struck out for the Eastern side of town – having forgotten to send that, perhaps meaningless, courtesy text. The steaming reusable felt heavy and hot in his hand, as he…one foot and then the other, moved.

<u>10</u>

Singed by a song - Gregorian,
Wanted and not want of those sins or virtues,
Grease and tortoiseshell pin-bull halving, lying on
that cape
Matte sprawling at the door of the Pyramid tent,
Underwent, and carved below, the bleak surface of the
Phoenix rise, brazen – bold as the ions that fail as yet
to
Unite us, yet underground beasts stay blind.

Our protagonist was next seen sidling down the
passageway, almost subterreranean-tunnel like, towards
Rafique's. He was at no.77, off this dusky passageway,
along one of the many side streets of Felltown, littered
with crisp packets and cigarette boxes.
The green, mottled and scarred door, swung open on
Grant's approach, seemingly because of a helpful breeze.

Rafique, sat on his once majestic and now dated sofa,
right on the brink of lighting up a particularly big phat
one. The lighter gripped in his deep-brown mitt.

Grant shot straight into the kitchen and put the kettle on.

Smoke billowed from the living room, a thick opaque
plume. Moments later, Grant returned with a small
beaker of herbal; found Rafique, almost in the same
position, gazing intently at a wall-hanging opposite.

"How is it, mate?" said the former.

"This one," said Rafique, indicating his smoke, smoothly "It's good, my man, ya it's good."
"Nice, well shall we put the racing on or something, something to ignore?" said Grant, grabbing the remote. Rafique simply nodded.
"You know, man, I often think this town becoming too liberal, too insulated, too infused with guilt 'know, for the have-nots", emitted Rafique.
"Yeah," Grant roughly agreed, settling down with a sip as the TV came on.
The herb started to take effect, and Grant through second-hand proximity, started to feel a bit dizzy and hazy – as the horses seemed to blend and blur.
"I saw that girl, d'other day, talking with that bullish crazy man, that Dune fella, that low-lord's henchman."
"You mean Tessa, and Mannal, why would they be speaking? That man's crazy, think it's his personal duty to protect the sanctity, nominal though it is, of the town, a one man mission to fight for the soul of a town that has none, or that sold it a long time ago, if that," said Grant.\
"Yeah man," said Rafique, a pause. "You know the teams at de top of the league this season?" an abrupt change of subject, but the herb was taking effect.
Grant pivoted "Yeah, the Long-Boatmen, the Fire Rangers and the Titans, isn't it?"
Rafique nodded, and grabbed a long mug of coffee at his side, swigged it generously, then went back to his reclined position.
As if possessed by a spirit, he suddenly went on: "I have the Titans to finish top, the Long-Boatmen second, what de yee reckon G-boy?" His pet name for Grant.

Grant was deep in thought, having suddenly remembered Tessa's name mentioned – why was she talking to Lord Ricka's bloodthirsty hound? He thought she was a purely trustworthy and benevolent person? It didn't add up.

Some time passed, with Rafique becoming more and more intent and invested in a pale ale 6-pack he had loaded down the side of the sofa.

His eyes crossed from the American Football on the TV, to his beer stash, and back and not once did he speak. Grant simply surveyed, and occasionally sipped, his herbal tea, which was going cold, and needed a refill.

"You're not one for café culture, eh Rafique?" he said bravely, as Rafique's gaze swerved back to his pale ale stash.
"Nah, not me, mon, bit decadent eh, that affluent café culture, eh, for all them insulated, liberal Babylonian types", he finished with a "And no mistake" and tapped out the ash of his funky cigarette.
"Yeah, indeed, Rafique, but it's nice to be seen, out and about, isn't it? Not squirreled or hidden away in a dusky drug den", said Grant. Rafique passed him the latest herbal stick, its ember close to going out, seemingly oblivious.
"Take this, mon, you'll smoke it and see it my way."

*

<u>11</u>

The battle at the beginning,
And a gripped lapel, fierce as fire –
Devil's eyes finding each other defiant,
An affront you see, an insult, an imposition;
Yes maybe imagined, as the pixies and ravens hold the
dell
Out there in the woods, things are deathly quiet, quiet
as death itself.

As the dust settled on another crazy week in old
Felltown, Grant settled into his chillman™ armchair in
the confines of his Man-cave.

Mannal Dune kicking off; his strange alliance with Tessa
Hartley – her continued ignorance and yet total seeming
cognizance of Grant's advances; the 'run-in' with
Melanie Funtumble; Areo Nort (Rambabast) the brave,
and handsome, explorer, rolling into town; more
lackadaisical 'sitting off' with his pals Dellus and
Rettison; a rather typical hang-out with Rafique
O'Shaughnessy at his man-cave, culminating of course in
getting rather high on the latest fungal acquisition.

Not to mention his ongoing rendezvous with Soothsay,
in her dusky peace and love yurt in the woods – the
purposes of which Grant was yet to ascertain, fully or
truly.

*

Later that very evening, Grant was settling in to his own
private ale stash, when a strange surge overcame him, a
feeling of pain and lust: the dangerous magnetism
between him and "that" Mel Funtumble. Chance had
brought them into each other's arms sure, and a nice
dose of Whiskey Alpha, but he couldn't shake the strange
sensation that it would lead him off track – distract him
from Tessa – lead him by this or another other means
into the abyss. An abyss he wasn't sure he could return
from – an abyss, he conceded, he had been disastrously
in before.

Glancing to the left and gripping his phone, he quickly group-text'd Dellus and Rettison. A brief wait in which he contemplated his strong, hazy pale… Ping! They were at St. Viv's. Trying to get some of that religion, he presupposed. Or trying to get some of her homemade vegan cakes. It mattered not; they were waylaid: more than probably for the foreseeable.

St. Viv was a colleague of old Soothsay, and Grant was fairly sure she'd had dealings with Robert, Soothsay's current Hercules, before. Formidable as she was kind, unyielding as she was adaptable, fair as she was downright severe, and beautiful in that austere way sometimes older women get to.
A fierce imperiousness lay about her aura.
*

Dellus was prone to seeking solace, and caffeine gratis, in the confines of St. Viv's church come boarding house. He often dragged himself there, when worn out with the degrading vissictitudes of the town, or burnt out by the lads' various fun but unwise escapades in the town. Rettison himself, a simple type, was more likely just attracted by the rosy glow of St. Viv's – both the person and the place, a place he could let his tough exterior fall away.

*

That latest soiree with Rafique had really knocked your protagonist for six. The fungal agent had followed the herbal additive, as it was getting to be that time of year – and a run-in with some fairly ardent pixies and fairies and gnomes had left him with quite a bit to contemplate. Grant knew of Bad Jon's involvement in his ill-advised liaison with Melanie Funtumble. The details of which he wasn't sure of because intoxicated; and he was fairly sure, if he asked Bad Jon, who'd be on a hiatus from one of his many inter-dimensional fights/robbing missions, that man would be equally as unsure, perhaps even more so.

Clear as a bell, in mind and body, Tessa contacted her friends and walked out with them in the evening air of Felltown. Mel, and "the other one", loyally flanking her, they popped into the Garrulous Lizard, who did a late opening – for decaffs and alcohol replacements exclusively – on evenings like this.

Clutching their recently acquired vegan sourdough loaves, and picking out some sweet treats of the organic, gluten-free variety, the ladies were content in their lot – and gleefully oblivious to the attentions of the man-folk in the rather desultory looking evening-lit café.

*

Areo Nort-Rambabast, the handsomely brave, was regaling someone with his latest adventure, from which a bestseller would be written entitled The Nort Star, up the South West face of the biggest mountain in the world, when in walked Bad Jon Diamond. Though to say walked, would be generous. It was more of a stumble, as if from a hedge, backwards.

*

<u>12</u>

A lone figure stood on the edge of the ridge they called Skyie Head. The glowing spire of St. Viv's was, well, glowing in the umber distance. The dance of stars was beginning, as what looked like a half moon appeared out the back of a dusky, obstructive cloud. Dellus Gently clutched one-and-a-half 4-packs of the strongest cider he could find in his sweaty, clammy mitt. He thought he'd find him here – yet again in one of his trances, the glorious pillock.

*

Grant appraised Dellus, and then took one of the large cans of cider – fruitlessly muttering 'cheers' as he cranked the ringpull. Another day in paradise, he thought and biffed his can against Dellus'. Yet another day.

*

PART TWO – DEFT

Chapter 13

And lo! It took but a brigand to bring you here, sparks

*Fly off the mangy cur, as the drift of flotsam petals lay
pebble-like*

On the distinct yet distant floor:

*You in brave denouement, sired of the north,
sacrificed yourself*

*Beneath that dusky and skeletal flag, so limp and
tattered now – The dark and*

*dirk, holding you as high champion; through the thorn
and thick*

Of bleak remembered east (you)

*Could have guessed there'd be a sudden, sultry end to
this once tidy scene –*

Maybe, love is all sad.

Lord Ricka, fond though he was of claiming overall jurisdiction of Felltown, did have his antecedent: Regio Dorsas, the right Hon, and a formidable force in the lordly realm, just like Lord Ricka, a local chieftain of sorts.

Regio did not rely on faithful henchman or hounds to do his bidding, unlike the erstwhile Bockley, but undertook and administered his matters first-hand and directly out in public with the 'beige masses'. Ricka had always maintained that his rival Dorsas simply liked the attention and lapped it up like some cartoon Lion.

Regio, more of a colour-sergeant than a chief in truth, knew of the comings and goings of the town: Grant's predicament for example, but through first-hand witnessing, as he often out in the café haunts and quaint nightspots of Felltown's rather dingy and small-fry excuse for a lively social scene.

Regio was frequently seen drinking at Bar Nun, albeit in the hours leaning towards closing – the "wee small" 9 and 10 onwards – and it was many an hour he spent there propping up the bar, sipping his dark brown ale devotedly, regaling the barkeepers, and holding court in a leonine fashion it must be said that infuriated Ricka Bockley, the latter being prone to easily-riled ire.

It was claimed, furthermore, that Tessa Hartley was his daughter, or his adopted daughter, or his goddaughter; notwithstanding the given name her ascendant position in the town itself attested much to his influence, and the rather worldy aspect his presence lent to, in particular, the female denizens of the domain.

<u>14</u>

A quagmire of antecedents,
And yet the man's a rock;
Finding it first of all, and thus she takes stock,
Limbic and hijacked, luminal and unpacked,
Caustic in deathly swamp, unseized, and caught out
in black cold –
Yet still, he holds oh so firm.

"And your friends. All thoroughly deserving of the praise they heap upon themselves, to a man", said Soothsay, icily.

<u>15</u>

The sable-haired, duskily skinned maiden passed by the window. Grant, temporarily enchanted by a book called The Island of Poig, spied her instantly and made for the shop door, as he dropped the dusty tome penned by one T L Skinner.

Declan and Eaglin's was a fanciful, some would say
frivolous, arts 'n crafty, vintage, 'any old stuff' bookshop.
Ran by the Irish husband and the French wife – it was
widely regarded in Felltown as a good place to hide/kill
the empty aeons of time and also as a good place to get
an eye on the outflow of Jovial Lane, right on the
intersection of Halcyon Avenue.

Grant Mosalgron veered out of the shop, throwing
Declan, who was fondling a small coiffed hamster who
lay on the desktop, a quick wave. The Irishman did not
look after Grant as he left, but merely continued stroking
the hamster, and took a sip of his chai latte.

As Grant emerged, Tessa was rounding the corner, hair
and scarf pulled up tight against the strong Westerly
wind. He took one brief look back at Declan and Eaglin's
tattered store-front and pursued apace.

<u>16</u>

Living as ghost not, that
Red hair tight bun, leading right to the traffic lights
With a fickle, flimsy stop,
Still grace with musty, clustered doldrum claimed
Cannot surrender – as blessed like fighters' grip, it
holds the lit pulse,
Bright as diamond, light as emerald.

"Got any plans?" the clerk said to him, as he handed over the change for Grant's shop-bought, Luke-warm 4 – pack of beers. Grant considered this for a moment, the words momentarily painting themselves in neon on the inside of his skull. Plans. It was 9:34 at night. He had just acquired 4 of the best beers he could, at this time of night. What he was going to do, he could hardly constitute as a "plan". He wouldn't credit it with the sophistication of a "Plan". He was going to go home, drink these 4 beers, and then pass out like he normally did. It was 9:34 at night – not the time for a plan – some would say too late for a "plan".
He chuckled to himself, and did not answer. Grant shoved the precious 4-beers roughly into the bag he had brought along for the purpose – perhaps that had been a plan (but Grant wouldn't credit himself with such indulgence) and left the shop.
Just for a bit.

Brandished his almond croissant, brandished a dirty turnip, Jon once was again out in the open, wheeling a skateboard with a crate strapped to it, behind him, the crate filled with red wine and cleaning chemicals.

<u>17</u>

Grant was contemplating the merits of his liaison with Melanie Funtumble, sitting on a bench in District Park alone, and watching the starlings in their murmur. I would NOT do it again, ever, he thought. I would NOT. But, he reasoned, if he had "done it again", and latterly found out about the event, he wouldn't exactly regret it: couldn't guarantee that the offence would not be repeated. On paper, though, in theory he would NOT do it again.

*

<u>18</u>

It was later that day. "I used to be pretty rock 'n roll",
said Grant, to Dellus and Rettison. "You still are",
proffered Dellus "Grant mate no one can touch you with
your wild exploits of the past, they're local legend", he
said as Areo Nort strode past the window, purposefully.
The three of them exchanged a meaningless look, as he
stalked off around the corner of the Gormless Flamingo
(a rival to the Garrulous Lizard kitsch coffee shop), and
then Grant returned to his reflective musing whilst
Dellus brandished his organic fair-trade croissant at
Rettison and said: "How's it going with that redhead, the
one who cannot be named, you know, stunner 'the other
one', mate of Tessa's?".
"She's called Felicity Snugglehard", said Rettison, with
resignation.
It turned out she was called Felicity Snugglehard.
Though Flic for short. Not breaking news, not a
newsflash, but a development from across the aisle, so to
speak, nonetheless Grant noted, and musingly took a sip
of his coffee. He was also glad news had not got back to
them about Melanie Funtumble, yet.

<u>19</u>

"What do you imagine happens", said Soothsay Brandelbaeke, from the confines of her dusky tent-cabin in the hushed woods.

"Well, I say her name, then she says my name, and then…Something happens", replied Grant, his own nebulous obscurity irritating him. "It goes 'Tessa', 'Grant' and then, something happens". He was convinced of it, though he wasn't convinced she knew his name, or that such acknowledgement or assent was likely.

"And you can't specify what?" said Soothsay, voice oozing like double cream.

<u>20</u>

Bad Jon had had a run-in with some of the worst-lot, two black eyes and a cracked, painful rib, and as such he was on the war-path. The cut-throat's blood was up.

<u>END OF PART TWO – PART THREE</u>

PART THREE – BEREFT AND BEYOND THE CLEFT?

Chapter 21

"You are full of such cant, Sir", the man in Grant's TV programme said, with a pompous finality. Period Drama. Mainstay. "Much cant", he repeated, bewigged and bespectacled, firmly right. Grant chuckled, and turned over. He loved these old words, long words, words complex and fallen off – words that those "normal" human beings simply dismissed as either a) spells b) complicated nonsense. Yet, it was true, Grant was sure, that such words had a definitive, and definite deliciousness; and though they might belong to the old world – Grant did well to keep them alive, even for his dead old Grandfather's sake.

He switched over, glanced at his smart-screen and looked out of the window; it was the strangest of new days – sunny and gloomy in equal measure, with the strongest of strong Westerlies blowing everything around on a sixpence. More to do, where to go?

22

So Grant went to see Soothsay Brandelbaeke again. And thus with heavy heart rounded the corner of the fence and wall and hopped into her yurt cabin.

Almost immediately, Soothsay called his name, and bade him sit on the little patchwork padded stool that lay beside her low-lying palatial throne.

"The chariot", Soothsay said, pulling a tarot card from her sleave – as Grant's eyes fixed on her – and holding it in front of his face with a soothing fluidity. As she did so, another card fell from her sleave, which she did not appear to know was there, and Grant caught a brief glance of 'The Hierophant' on its face, before it was briefly tucked away into the green and gold folds of Soothsay's current visage.

"You must pursue your goals with single-minded focus, young Grant" she said, holding the card once more so it hovered in the yurt-cabin's gloomy light. He gave it a quick look, and settled once more back into his stool, content for now, as this was what he wanted to hear. "Simply do not falter, do not sway, do not slide", implying the fates would guide him.

As she filled her tobacco pipe, Grant looked around the walls of the tent once again, and your hero tried his best to remember that all this 'woo', Astro-tarot stuff she espoused was inevitably useful to him, and impossible to ignore. He did his best to always focus on the guidance he was getting, and the utility it could cause in his life.

"Anyway," Soothsay said, lighting up, "You've been making progress, out of the gloom and into the Sun's solar embrace", very good young man, her eyes seemed to say – and although he didn't entirely believe her, he trusted the deep wisdom of the ancients, the elders who she represented.

<u>23</u>

As before, this day held strange promise, a wind like a hurricane blowing everything up, the weather as changeable as the astrology, as Soothsay had noted.

Grant was in front of a vivid poster on a lamppost mid-way down Jovial Road.
"Qorrza Howl, Exciting Alt-Rock Post-Punk 6-piece Outfit" it read it big bold red letters – and underneath in smaller, more delicate letters, the time and location of the gig. It was this Saturday coming, in the roustabout garden of The Mucky Stable, a bar Grant rarely frequented, unless he was 'on tour' with Dellus and Rettison, but still the signal of the gig enticed him. The prospect of a night-out to savour cooled his heart for a moment, and then a flash of gold-auburn hair caught his eye, and he turned to see Tessa, illuminated across the street from him, carrying a paper bag.

She was alone, at this very moment, no Mel or Flick as flankers or guardians.

Just as he took a step towards her, a car went by with 'Buffalo Soldier' emitting faintly from deep-bass speakers; as he scuttled across the road, Grant briefly noticed that it was Rafique in the driving seat..
"I", he made to speak to her, as with his right foot he closed the gap, "I was wondering", still not certain, his eyes wandering to her, and hers just beginning to focus. "I was wondering if you wanted to go to this, punkish, gig this Saturday night – Quorza Howl – it looks like me and the boys will be going?", Grant said.
She looked him up and down. Even though he was 2 or 3 inches taller than her, he felt small in her presence – as she appraised and assessed him thoroughly. Terrified of the consequences now he had bridged the gap, Grant simply stared back and tried to look resolute, unflinching, and even quietly impressive.

"Sure", she said. "Me and the girls/ladies were thinking of going to that anyway, let the hair down...We won't be drinking though, Flic's on antibiotics, and Mel thinks she may be up the duff", Tessa went on.

Grant flinched more a moment, but knew he must respond. "Sure indeed," he echoed, "Me and the lads will get there for 7:30, I think the gig should start by then, but it's doors at 7pm" trailing off, wondering if was boring her with details
"Ace", she said, and turned to go, and for a moment Grant thought of grasping her arm and preventing her from turning off out his sight down Rembrandt Grove, but thought better of it, and returned his lover's gaze to his 7.3 hazelfoam™ monkey, purchased a few hours earlier.
She went on with a flutter of silken blue.

<u>24</u>

Robert, Brandelbaeke's beau and paid-up safe pair of hands, was remonstrating with Mannal Dune. Bad Jon stripped to the waist, and barefooted, was wielding a cricket bat menacingly behind Robert. The latter was indeed giving Mannal a dressing down, holding him by the lapels of his rather-jarring Hawaiian shirt. They were in the district park, beside the Cricket ground. It was not known how Jon had acquired the cricket bat, but he growled ferociously as Robert's words seemed to fall on deaf ears with the madman. Mannal, for his part, looked maliciously from Robert to Jon with eyes as cool as icy steel.

Regio Dorsas, who was happenchance walking his long-haired collie with the David Bowie eyes through the park, surveyed the action, and went perchance to intercede, though his impression at first manifested as inaccurate. Thinking at first that Robert was in the right, he quickly decided that the latter was interrupting the 'natural flow' of life, 'disturbing the natural order', even 'halting evolution' and biffed Robert on the back of the head from behind.

Things quickly became savage.

*

Vociferously, Grant was rifling through the copy of T L Skinner's work he had acquired from Declan and Eaglin's – a children's story, full of faeries and demons though it was, he was convinced he could glean and acquire some knowledge from it, so devoured it hungrily. It was 2 days till Saturday, he was pondering deeply the next move and how he would approach his meeting with Tessa and his friends. Text from Rettison: he was on his way back from the farm. Too early to get drunk, at this point, surely?!

*

Areo Nort-Rambabast, passed over the glossy book, signed and sealed, to the anticipating fan, and smiled smugly, his job done. One of two middle-aged women on the other table, muttered "so brave and handsome" under her breath, and the smile became wider. His book, 'All or Nortin,', was his seminal, gripping work, just released, detailing his climb up the Western face of every known mountain in less than five hours, was the talk of the café lobby and its patrons.

"Well, I think I'll have another deluxe hot chocolate", "organic" he added for effect to the waiting shop clerk. He had only meant to stay a week, but this Felltown place was warming to him.

<h1 style="text-align:center"><u>25</u></h1>

A sturdy wingspan,
Surprising strong paw on a robust snout,
Orbs glimmering with all the gleam of a mystery,
untold
Found scheming like foul wizards at the river twixt –
the fold
Old and odd, callous as a track-list wanting a God,
you want for nothing as
It all comes across.

A cold and dusty wind blew over the archipelago of
Felltown, even though the sun's rays shone, seeming
ineffective, as bold Areo Nort walked stridently to St.
Viv's.

*

So as Grant was readying himself for the gig, Quorza
Howl, this Saturday night – he prepared his outfit,
flannel, dark jeans, discrete man-bag, and his
accoutrements – vape, paracetemol, auxiliary pack of
chewing gum – he was quietly confident that things
would go well with Tessa, Mel, et al. The days preceding
had gone by quite uneventful: more trips to the
Garrulous Lizard, secondary and tertiary trips to
Soothsay Brandelbaeke (with Robert in tow, sporting a
black-eye) for guidance and encouragement, and his
usual permissive patrols to Skyie Head and St. Viv's. Yet
still he uttered a few words to the warden he passed on
the street, and remained confident.

As a light flickered on in the flat opposite, he reasoned to
himself that as a Mosalgron from a long line, of
Mosalgrons, his preparedness was his defining trait.
Dellus Grainge, or Dylan, for his sins was known for his
louche laziness; Rettison was for his hardy work-ethic
but total inability to commit to social situations. Grant,
for all his flaws, was prepared; immersively prepared. It
was 4pm.

3 hours till lift off.

*

Grant was in the club, though not outside at the Mucky
Stable, but on the dingy top floor, currently sluicing the
porcelain.

As he came down, and emerged once again into the garden, he spotted Dellus, sporting what looked like a smoothie, or might have been a Mocktail, and he muttered to himself "silly Billy". The band was indeed great, just the tonic for the indecisive weather – powerful, punchy and unequivocal, and Rettison was having a great time. The big chap was right near the front, head-banging happily and swigging a big Stein of beer. Mel and Flic had currently evinced themselves, and were off in the bathroom no doubt powdering hungry noses – but Tessa stood alone where Grant, your hero, had left her.

He took out a quick chewing gum, and produced his vape as he approached: blowing a big cloud of smoke, so as he came before he emerged like Zorro or some fabled ancient hero. He wasn't that, and to be honest he just didn't his 'Nic' hit, but appear he did, and she seemed impressed merely that he was still standing.

"Good piss?" she said.
"Yep," he firmly assented, and took her by the hand finally. It was nearly 9, he had wanted to do this all night, but things had taken some loosening, smoothening – and now his blood was sufficiently up to roll the dice, make his move.

*

<u>26</u>

Readying himself
Underwent with the totality of life,
A fullness thriving in full release…

Areo Nort had indeed arrived at St. Viv's and weighed anchor, 3 copies of his new bestseller safely tucked in his Scandinavian rucksack. St Viv herself met him with jocular warmth: she always loved to hear war stories from beyond the town; tales of derring do reminded of the cost and consequences of risky adventure beyond the fringes of what she so dearly stewarded and kept safe. Her helper, Lilibet, gratefully accepted a copy of Areo's tome, pre-signed of course, and he sat down with a grin to a hearty and hale bowl of vegetable stew and an on-the-house spiced mug of latte.

<u>27</u>

Mist is silent splendor, above tors of cannon creep and
thicker fastness,
Sun splaying the cobbles, with
Deep green fields unexplored – marv'ling at the
madness, unkept by roar…

The band were finishing. With one riotous howl, Quorza Howl sent one last soaring note of rock attitude into the air and the Mucky Stable erupted.

Tessa grabbed Grant's hand, and with one quick
movement, they faced each other, and their lips met.
Warmth, luscious warmth, delicious fragrance, a soft,
unfurling intoxication of deadly warmth…

And then he blacked out.

*

<u>28</u>

Singed with silent sadness: a song born in the
unspoken moments,
Keeping time with the watch-worn, readily – no war
to be called to
As the red orb rises, once more it's Kingdom come…

Grant had brief, blurry recognition of a motorbike, a
horse, a chariot, a journey through a large, long
woodland – and somehow he had ended up here.

Where was here? He was stooped, standing but his joints
all cramped, catching his breath – his eyes weren't open
but he could feel the darkness surrounding him, and he
couldn't slow his heartbeat for the life of him.

"Open", came a voice.

Grant opened his eyes, and was met with the interior of some sort of dusky cave, with a man of tall stature, his face shrouded with blacks and browns and greys, standing at the back. The man, if man he was, was backed by strange figures, which faded in and out of focus, dark blue and green, flittering in the source-less light. Their huge eyes protruded, bulging, and receded, and they chattered, behind the tall man, as if out of loyalty.

"You have come."
"Why am I here, who are you?" said Grant.

But the man was chanting, and he had on his chest, Grant just noticed, a large blue symbol, glowing, like a Rune. Grant eventually took a long breathe in, and gave two quick exhales, and then his pattern eased. He looked at the man again and asked,
"Who are you?"
"In life I was called Mylan Morrigan, now I am something else, something different", he said.
Your hero stood up straighter, and pierced the man with a firmer look.
"Where are we, somewhere near Avonnis Wood? And further to that, who are you really? Some connection to Felltown, were you married to that woman, that woman who went away…Elizabeth?"
"Elizabeth Bockley, yes. I was a great carpenter, a master woodsman, and I married that fake Lord Ricka's sister." He paused, stroking what might have been a long brown-grey beard in the darkness. "And it all came to naught, as this young one we have before us knows", he said to the chittering creatures behind him, who erupted in delicious delight.

*

Grant thought he saw faces amongst the creatures in the darkness, Areo Nort…Robert…Ricka Bockley…Flic Snugglehard…all except her, all except Tess.

"You must take this", said Mylan Morrigan.

A calloused hand reached across to Grant, bearing a dun metallic cup. Grant noticed that the hand looked like it had been ripped to shreds, then put back together untidily. It was full of some liquid, impossible to tell what colour.

"I drink this," proffered Grant.
"You drink this, and it all goes away. The death, the doom, the destruction,." said Morrigan.
"I drink this, and the lattes, the pub trips, the financial planning, the flirtations with waitresses, all of it?" Grant asked.
"You drink this, and all of it goes away, no more frustration, no more confusion, no more not knowing, or wishing you knew…this is the step. You can have everything back, or you can just have one thing", said Morrigan, voice deep and husky.

Grant drank, and hunched over. Instantly the cup flew out of his hand, and within a second his back straightened once again.
A tunnel opened up behind Mylan Morrigan's right, to Grant's left, and he said "On we go, time to leave everything behind…find nothing."

It's time, Grant thought, on and through, and took one step forward.

"That's the Game" said the Heterogon, "On."

On it was.

<u>END?</u>

<u>29 EPILOGUE</u>

Sharp intake as a great emergence
Few breaths to get over line
Ping! goes phone: Mel is pregnant with twins
Reaching mitt, as deep lunge to regain balance

Large devil or shark: and she tells me her dream
Ping! Dellus doing yoga with Lilibet at St. Viv's:
Giving a sun-salutation;
Quiet as mice wandering shadows, Rettison quietly
Asks..

Long creep of yawning death
Too much to gain through holding back, but jump anyway,
Ping! Regio seen accosting that Bad Jon in corner Shop,

Jon quietly mutters the old Lion is playing chess with
Brandy

Long leash, short drop for the bold adventurer,
Cast asunder, by sultry tides from higher echelon –
Denied, crept soft through Dirt, that big white orb
Crowing – drowned by the omens he could never own;

And Soothsay, Ping! she's all alone, but never two
For the one, she loves, exists within a sunken shore
Return, at last, fair roving Robert, with Tessa by
Hand led.

END.

This book is dedicated to Orca the Cat, fierce companion and rodent-catcher to the Gods.